Queen Calafia – Th
Deciphering betwee
the Quee

Queen Calafia – The Real Wonder Woman

Deciphering between the Myth and Facts of the Queen of California
By: (Ishma'il) Marcus Allgood – ©2017

T.H.I.N.K. Publications

ISBN: 9798700463492
Imprint: Independently published

www.wanttherealtruth.com

Acknowledgment

Writing a book is harder than I thought and more rewarding than I could have ever imagined. None of this would have been possible without Melina Abdullah. It was her invites to the Black Lives Matter marches and rallies in California that lead to the discovery of our ancient African Queen.

I'm eternally grateful to my friend, Jose Osuna, of Home Boys Industries, who educated me about this Amazonia Queen. He introduced me to what real community organizing looks like versus activism (which is often reactionary).

To Ms. Saaudiah Muhammad, from the Nation of Islam, who so graciously allowed me to use a painting of her image (by Jean Philippe Roussel) to be the cover of my book. The painting to me captured the regal-ness and .class of an African queen. It says I am powerful, so don't mess with me. I had to have it. You are a queen in your own right, representing for us right there in Chicago. You had to have descended from royalty, I am convinced.

To my Ummi, my mother, Juliette Taylor, I love you my Nubian queen and thank you for always being the someone I could turn to during those dark and desperate years. You were abandoned and left alone at the Elyria Memorial Hospital with me as a baby, like the Egyptian Princess, Hagar. You could've aborted me, or gave me up for adoption. But you kept me even through the struggle. That is why I go by the name Ishma'il, in honor of that struggle. You are my Queen. Mom - you sustained me in ways that I never knew that I needed.

And last but not least. I would like to thank the most High God, who is known by many beautiful names. Because without you I couldn't exist. And thank you for your Grace and Mercy, and for Blessing me with much more than I deserve. Thank you.

Table of Contents

Acknowledgment   2

Introduction   6

1. They Came Before Columbus   10
   - Gold Spears: 10
   - Cape Verde Islands   12
   - King Cotton   13
   - African Ocean Currents   15
   - The Moors in Pre-Columbus America   17
   - Proclamation by a Turkish President   17
   - Dr. Barry Fell Claims   20
   - Mansa Musa & Family   22

2. The Adventures of Esplandián   25
   - A Rough Outline of Calafia's story   27
   - Amazons, FACT or FICTION?   30
   - Black Amazons   32
   - Diodorus Siculus   32
   - Libya is Africa   34
   - The Sauromatians   39
   - Dahomey Amazons   42
   - The Damute and Gorage Amazons   44
   - Amazons in America   51

	A Women Caliph in America?	55
	• Left Behind (in America)	56
	• Queens of the Islamic lands	59
	• War in Constantinople	61
	• The Sultanate of Women	62
	• The Island Paradise Filled With Gold	66
	• Origins of the American Amazons	73
	• Mythical language of the Griffin	79
	• Protoceratops	80
	• Egyptian vulture	86
3.	The Legacy of Calafia	90
	• Calafia In Pop Culture	90
	• Calafia In Psychology	91
	• Strong Black Womanhood	98
	Thank You	101
	Haiku Poem	102
4.	Other Books by the Author:	103
5	Bibliography	104

The Queen Calafia statue located at the Watts Labor Community Action Committee (WLCAC) premise in California.

Introduction

I moved to California back in the summer 2013. I kept hearing about this African Queen that founded California (according to legend). I didn't hear about her from Black folks, but heard about her primarily from Latinos. I thought that this was intriguing, that the state may have been founded by a Black woman, and secondly that I was hearing about it from Mexican-Americans. Fast forwarding a bit, I was participating in a Black Lives Matter March in March 2017 in Watts California. It was the anniversary of the death of Wakiesha Wilson, who was killed while in police custody. Although I am not an official member of "Black Lives Matter", however, I do support the movement and I am an ally.

Regarding the Wakiesha Wilson case, the prosecutors declined to pursue charges in her case, and authorities say she hanged herself in a Los Angeles jail cell, saying there was *"insufficient evidence proving anyone was criminally responsible for her death.*[1]*"* This really upset the Black community. Black Lives Matter and the mother of Wakiesha Wilson took the position that she was murdered because there was sufficient evidence to say that she did NOT kill herself. *"An attorney representing Wilson's family"*

---

[1] Los Angeles Times: " Prosecutors: No 'criminal liability' in controversial case of woman who died in LAPD jail cell" by Kate Mather Contact Reporter.July 10, 2017

previously "*said there were no signs Wilson was distraught when she spoke to relatives on the phone after her arrest and again the following morning, about 90 minutes before her death. She made plans to call them later in the day during their Easter celebration and talk to her 13-year-old son, attorney Jaaye Person-Lynn said*"[2]. What does Queen Calafia have to do with this?

Well, while we were matching for Wakiesha Wilson we came to this community center in Watts, and there was this beautiful statue of this tall regal Black Woman there, with cornrows in her hair, and with her standing on top of the world. I inquired about her, and people stated that this was Queen Calafia, the original ruler of California. It seemed sort of Ironic, we were there matching for a Black Queen and walked up on a statue of a Black queen. I wanted to research more about her.

---

[2] Los Angeles Times: "Family questions circumstances surrounding death of woman in LAPD jail cell" by Kate Mather Contact Reporter. April 5, 2016

Further incentive to actually complete this project was prompted by a discussion I had with Jose Osuna from Home Boy Industries in September 2017. He and Damond Johnson, AKA Mustapha, were both there at Home Boys doing great work in the community, turning ex-felons and gang bangers into productive citizens by helping them get an education, and jobs. We were all out there supporting Home Boy's 5K marathon race in support of Compton High school.

Jose brought it up to me that the Moors and Queen Calafia were here in California before Columbus. Jose recounted visiting the Smithsonian Museum display of Native Americans in Washington DC, and many of them were very dark skinned, akin to Black Americans. This conversation brought to mind the research within Ivan Van Sertima's book, "*They Came Before Columbus*". So I thought, "There has to be something to this." It seems very plausible that queen Calafia existed if there were Africans here in America before Christopher Columbus. So let's start there.

1. They Came Before Columbus

- **Gold Spears:**

Ivan Van Sertima, in his book[3] about the presence of Africans in America, he refers to a book trilogy published in 1903 by John Boyd Thatcher [4] which deals with all the diaries, voyages, journals of Christopher Columbus. And Thatcher points

They Came Before Columbus: The African Presence of Early America" By Ivan Van Sertima,

---

[3] "They Came Before Columbus: The African Presence of Early America" By Ivan Van Sertima, (1976) from Random House.

[4] Christopher Columbus, His Life, His Works, His Remains, together with an Essay on Peter Martyr of Anghera and Bartolomé de las Casas, the first Historians of America (two volumes, 1903)

out that on Columbus's second voyage, Native Americans of Haiti told him that Black people came there in large boats from the South and the South East, trading with them with Gold Tip medal spears. Columbus did not believe them so he sent samples of these gold tip spears back to Spain. And the experts in Spain concluded that these spear tips had the same ratio of Gold, Silver, and Copper alloys as those made in Africa Guinea, which is in West Africa near Sierra Leone.

The following was documented in the Nuova Raccolta[5], part I, volume I: *"Columbus wanted to find out what the Indians of Espanola had told him, that had come from the south and southeast, [N]egro people who brought those spear points made of a metal which they call guanin, of which he had sent samples to the king and queen for assay and*

---

[5] Christopher Columbus The Journal - Nuova Raccolta Colombiana English Edition; Volume 1 Part 1 and Part 2 Published by Instituto Poligrafico F. Zecca Dello Stato Libreria Dello Stato, Rome, 1992

which was found to have 32 parts – 18 of gold, 6 of silver, and 8 of copper.[6]

- **Cape Verde Islands**

Furthermore, the Portuguese told Columbus upon his return from his first voyage, that they were aware of Negroes from the Cape Verde islands in Africa, and that they travelled far to the west with merchandise in large boats. There are two things to bear in mind here:

> **1.)** The Portuguese were aware of African navigation because they, the Portuguese, have been around in Africa since about 1415. In fact they had clashes with the Gambia Navy. This confirms that Africans had shipping capabilities.
>
> **2.)** The Portuguese were aware of a land mass that was in the south as a result of African movements.

---

[6] Ivan Van Sertima, "Evidence For An African Presence in Pre-Columbian America," in Ivan Van Sertima (ed.) <u>African Presence in Early America</u>, New Brunswick, Transaction Publishers, 1992, p.30.

Christopher Columbus who married a Portuguese woman that spoke of a fort built by Portuguese in 1482 in Ghana or Gold Coast, known as Saint George of Mina. Therefore the Portuguese, including his wife, would have been aware of such movements by Africans to the Americas. In fact Columbus and his brother tried to get the Portuguese to fund their voyage across the Western Ocean before they received finance from Spain.

- **King Cotton**

Ivan Van Sertima asserts that, not only do we have the documents of the Portuguese, Columbus himself, and the oral traditions of the Native Americans themselves that say Africans were there in America BEFORE Columbus. We also have the testimonies of Spanish medal experts that said the metal tips of the spears traded with the Native Haitians were African. But they also found the same kind of cotton (Gossypium.hirsutum) in the Cape Verde Islands that was also in the Americas. They thought initially it was African in origin, brought to the Americas by the

Portuguese prior to Columbus, but the eugenics expert found that it originated in the Caribbean Islands and was brought to West Africa pre-Columbus[7]. Therefore there is evidence of trade between Africans and Native Americans prior to Columbus.

---

[7] Contact And Exchange in the Ancient World. University of Hawaii Press. Edited by Victor H. Mair, pg 250

- **African Ocean Currents**

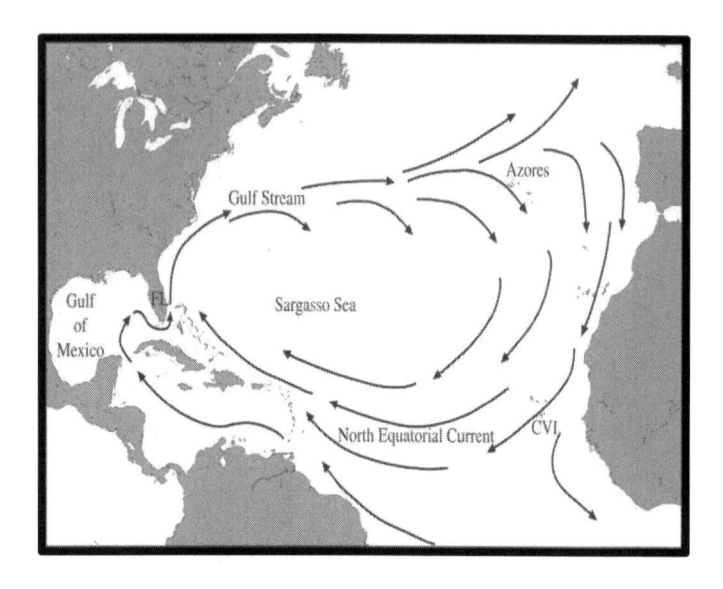

Schematic of the North Atlantic Subtropical Gyre and study area. Arrows indicate the generalized direction of current flow. Currents and locations discussed in the text are identified. FL marks Florida, USA; CVI marks the Cape Verde Islands.

Experts have discovered there are three major currents in Africa, about 100 miles off of the African Coast that take you straight to America[8]. Once you get caught in those

---

[8] The Journal of The Royal Society Interface: Tracking the long-distance dispersal of marine organisms: sensitivity to ocean model resolution. By -

currents, even if you planned it or not, you automatically get swept to America. Anything that remains afloat, and not eaten by the fish, got pushed towards the Americas. Off the Cape Verde islands there is a current that takes you onto the Northern tip of South America into the Caribbean, into the Gulf of Mexico.

If you are coming off of the coast of Sana Gambia, the current there will take you to South America, into the Caribbean islands, and then into the Gulf of Mexico. If you are on the Southern Coast of Africa, the current there will carry you into South America and you can then fall into the currents that take you into the Caribbean islands into the Gulf of Mexico. There is even more evidence that suggests that Africans have been here in America even before 3 BC (Before Christ).

Nathan F. Putman, Ruoying He . Article Published 24 January 2013.DOI: 10.1098/rsif.2012.0979

- ## The Moors in Pre-Columbus America

The Princess of the Moors by Leonard Freeman

- ## Proclamation by a Turkish President

In a televised speech in Istanbul, Turkish President Recep Tayyip Erdogan claimed that Muslims had discovered the Americas three centuries before the voyages of Christopher Columbus. He was addressing a summit of Muslim leaders from Latin America.

"Contacts between Latin America and Islam date back to the 12th century. Muslims discovered America in 1178, not Christopher Columbus,"
Erdogan said. "Muslim sailors arrived in America from 1178. Columbus mentioned the existence of a mosque on a hill on the Cuban coast.[9]"

Christopher Columbus did admit in his papers that on Monday, October 21, 1492 CE while his ship was sailing near Gibara on the north-east coast of Cuba, he saw a mosque on top of a beautiful mountain[10]. I find it interesting that President Erdogan did not speak to their ethnicity but to their religion. And he omitted the fact that Africans have been coming here to America before there was such a thing as Muslim, Jew, or Christian. But the fact remains, to credit his point, the

---

[9] Washington Post, World View, Muslims discovered America before Columbus, claims Turkey's Erdogan. By Ishaan Tharoor November 15, 2014
[10] PRECOLUMBIAN MUSLIMS IN THE AMERICAS, By: Dr. Youssef Mroueh

Muslim Moors did come to America before Columbus.

- **Dr. Barry Fell Claims**

Dr. Barry Fell, a professor of invertebrate zoology at the Harvard Museum of Comparative Zoology, introduced in his book **'Saga America-1980'** with solid scientific evidence supporting the arrival of Muslims from North and West Africa centuries before Columbus. Dr. Fell discovered the existence of the Muslim schools at Valley of Fire, Allan Springs, Logomarsino, Keyhole, Canyon, Washoe and Hickison Summit Pass (Nevada), Mesa Verde (Colorado), Mimbres Valley (New Mexico) and Tipper Canoe (Indiana) dating back to 700-800 CE. And there engraved on rocks in the arid western U.S, he found texts,

Saga America - Maintains that complex, advanced societies flourished here before the arrival of Christopher Columbus, and uses coins, artwork, and other artifacts found across America to support these theories.

diagrams and charts representing the last surviving fragments of what was once a system of schools - at both an elementary and higher level. The language of instruction was North African Arabic written with old Kufic Arabic scripts. The subjects of instruction included writing, reading, arithmetic, religion, history, geography, mathematics, astronomy, and sea navigation. The descendants of the Muslim visitors of North America are members of the present **Iroquois, Algonquin, Anasazi, Hohokam and Olmec native people**[11]. So Jose Osuna was correct (See introduction), there were Black Native Indian Americans. And Dr. Fell also claims that many centuries before Christopher Columbus reached America, Celts, Basques, Phoenicians, Egyptians, and others were visiting North America also. These are all important points when we discuss Queen Calafia.

---

[11] THACHER,JOHN BOYD *Christopher Columbus,*New York 1950,P.380

- ## Mansa Musa & Family

Mansa Musa depicted holding a gold coin from the 1375 Catalan Atlas.

We heard of the great story of Sultan (king) of the West African Islamic empire of Mali named Mansa Musa (1312-1337 CE) where he gave away so much **Sadaqah** (charity) in gold, while on his voyage to Mecca, that it disrupted the world economy. What many of us may not have known is the fact that King Mansa Musa was protected by black, all female royal guards on his famous and influential hajj to Mecca in 1324 CE[12].

---

[12] Sabir, Wanda. "Wanda's Picks". San Francisco Bayview Nov 1, 2003.. * Interview with the curator of the African

On a side note, while King Musa was travelling to Mecca on his famous Hajj, he informed the scholars of the Mamluk Bahri sultan court (An-Nasir Nasir Edin Muhammad III-1309-1340 CE) in Cairo, that his brother, sultan Abu Bakari (1285-1312CE) had undertaken two expeditions into the Atlantic Ocean. When the sultan did not return to Timbuktu from the second voyage of 1311 CE, Mansa Musa became sultan of the empire[13]. Abu Bakari most likely had an all-female royal guard also on his travels. I will refer to this later on. (See section "Left Behind (in America)")

Even further, anthropologists have proven that the Mandinkas under Mansa Musa's instructions explored many parts of North America via the Mississippi and other rivers systems. At Four Corners, Arizona,

---

American Historical and Cultural Society Museum, John William Templeton.
https://web.archive.org/web/20031101082701/http://www.sigidiart.com/Docs/WandasPicksCalifia.htm
[13] CAUVET, GILES *Les Berbers de L'Amerique,* Paris 1912,P.100-101

writings show that they even brought elephants from Africa to the area.[14]

---

[14] COLUMBUS, FERDINAND *The Life of Admiral Christopher Columbus*, Rutgers Univ.Press, 1959, P.232

2. The Adventures of Esplandián

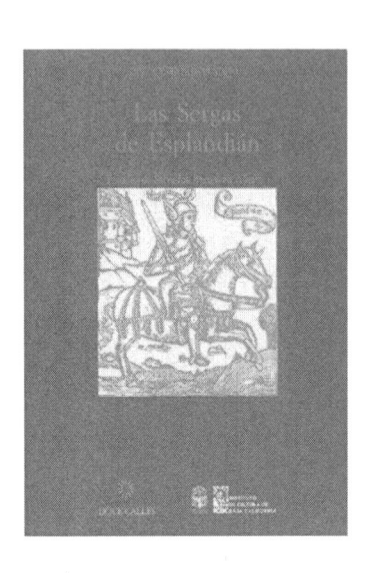

Las Sergas de Esplandián is a novel written by Garci Rodríguez de Montalvo in the late fifteenth or early sixteenth century. The novel is a sequel to a popular fifteenth century set of chivalric romance novels, Amadís de Gaula.

This lays down the groundwork of this article. The fact the Africans were here says that there is a possibility of an African Queen being here in America. There is this fictional book where Queen Calafia was mentioned by Spanish writer **Garci Rodríguez de Montalvo** called "*Las sergas de Esplandián*" (The Adventures of Esplandián), written around 1500. Although the account is fictional, I believe there are clues within the story that leads to the identity of the queen or to a tribe of Amazonia women in America.

When Rodríguez tells the story of this mythological Queen in his book, he mentions the story of Calafia as an intermission or a break in the narrative of *Esplandián*[15]. The majority of the book is about Esplandián's adventures, while his encounter with Queen Calafia is just one of many of his adventures. Calafia is introduced as this royal, regal, courageous, beautiful, very tall, strong Black woman *"full in the bloom of womanhood, the most beautiful of a long line of queens who ruled over the mythical realm of California"*. She is said to be *"desirous of achieving great things"*; and she wanted to see the world and plunder a portion of it with superior fighting ability, using her army of Amazon women warriors. She commanded a fleet of ships with which she demanded tribute from surrounding lands, and she kept an aerial defense force of griffins, fabulous animals which were **native to California**, trained to kill any man they found. (See section "Mythical Language of the Griffin")

---

[15] Putnam, Ruth (1917). Herbert Ingram Priestley, ed. *California: the name*. Berkeley: University of California. pg. 313

- **A Rough Outline of Calafia's story**

The rough outline of Calafia as she appears in Montalvo's book is thus:

Radiaro[16], a Muslim man, somehow makes it past the man-eating griffins and is granted an audience with Queen Calafia. *(Probably because they only eat dead bodies, because they are not Griffins, but I will talk about that later).* He requests aid from this pagan queen; because his home city of Constantinople was overtaken by Christian invaders and he needs help to fend them off. Queen Calafia, thinking now is as good a time as any for a fight, agrees to help him. She marshals her army of griffin-riding warrior women and they sail from California to Constantinople.

At first, Calafia's forces are successful, as the griffins gleefully snatch Christian men from the ramparts surrounding the city and destroy them. However, as the Muslim forces move in to take the city, the griffins don't stop.

---

[16] Lands of Promise and Despair: Chronicles of Early California, 1535–1846 edited by Rose, Marie Beebe, Robert M Senkewicz

They can only distinguish between male and female; they can't tell Christian from Muslim, and keep up the snatch-and-eat until the Muslims are forced to retreat and Calafia calls her griffins back.

Calafia's new strategy is to challenge the Christian king in Constantinople to a duel – single combat, winner-take-all. The King accepts, and brings his entourage out to meet Calafia and her entourage. There's a bit of love at first sight between Calafia and one of the king's sons, Esplandián himself. Calafia tries to show off and attract his attention, but Esplandián isn't interested in a pagan woman who doesn't know her place. (How offensive is that?)

However, the next day, Calafia and her buddy Radiaro fight king Amadis and his son Esplandián. Radiaro is defeated by Esplandián and Queen Calafia is beaten in battle by Amadis and taken prisoner. Not only is Calafia defeated, but she converts to Christianity, marries a knight named Talanque, who was Esplandián's cousin, and returns back to California with the intent of opening up the island to men. The story continues on without her, with Esplandián going on to other adventures. Although Montalvo's book is a fictional tale, Calafia and her Amazons captured the Spanish imagination, as *The Adventures of Esplandián* became wildly popular in Spain. I do believe much of the myth of Calafia is based on real African Women that lived in America before Columbus.

So some of the features of the story I will talk about on this article:

1. Amazons Fact of Fiction
2. Black Amazons
3. Amazons in America
4. A Woman Caliph in America
5. War in Constantinople
6. The Island of California
7. Mythical language of the Griffin

- ## Amazons, FACT or FICTION?

The Dahomey Amazons were frontline soldiers in the army of the Kingdom of Dahomey, a West African empire that existed from 1625 to 1894. Its remnants lie in modern-day Benin, which occupies a sliver of the coast between Nigeria and Togo.

Let's stop right there. Rodríguez de Montalvo's description of Calafia, her people, and her country was based upon many centuries of stories about Amazons, groups of women warriors who fought like men. Now the question is, "Did Amazon women really exist?" Many of the Greek historians like

Diodorus Siculus and Herodotus thought so. But in 1861 Johann Jakob Bachofen published his radical thesis that the Amazons were not a myth but a fact. In his view, humanity started out under the rule of womankind and only switched to patriarchy at the dawn of civilization[17]. There was, however, one major problem with the Bachofen-inspired theory of matriarchy: There was not a shred of physical evidence to support it. Thus the trail of the Amazons nearly went cold after Herodotus. However, there seems to be new evidence out there that the original Amazon women were in fact African which parallels the description of Queen Calafia being referred to as a Black Woman.

---

[17] The Amazon Women: Is there any truth behind the myth? Smithsonian Magazine, by Amanda Foreman April 2014

- **Black Amazons**

Depiction on a Greek vase of a negroid Amazon kneeling in front of an altar with a palm-tree, indicating that she was an African Amazon, from Libya

- **Diodorus Siculus**

Greek Historian Diodorus Siculus gives us an account of Dionysius of Mitylene, who, on his part, drew on Thymoetes, states that before the Amazons of the Thermodon (in Northern Turkey) there were, much earlier in time, the Amazons of Libya[18]. These Amazons started from Libya, passed through Egypt and Syria, and stopped at the Caïcus in Aeolis, near which they founded several cities.

There even exists a picture on a Greek vase which obviously shows a "negroid" Amazon kneeling in front of an altar. Behind the altar you can see a palm-tree, making it quite clear that the Greek artist depicted an African Amazon, from Libya. Palm trees in Italy are not part of the native fauna. The only palm trees native to the northern Mediterranean countries is the European fan palm[19].

---

[18] The Library of History of Diodorus Siculus, Book III, 52
[19] Your Ultimate Palm Tree Handbook by Darla Wotherspoon

- <u>**Libya is Africa**</u>

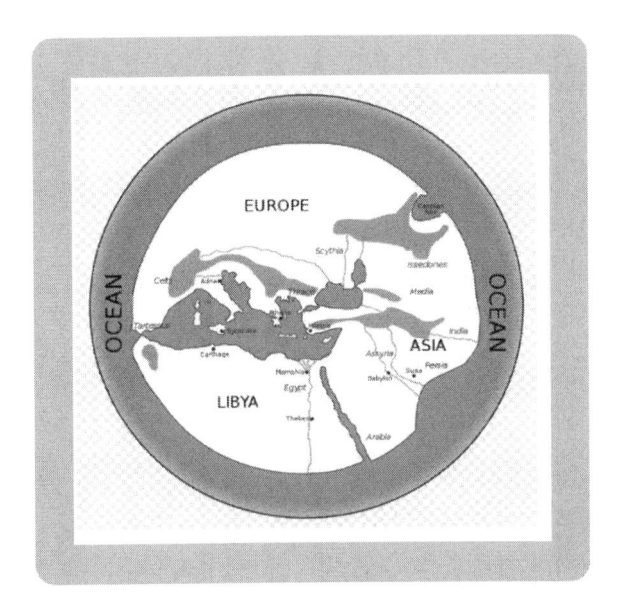

Reconstruction of Hecataeus' map

And when we speak of Libya, we are not speaking of the modern Libya of today (one country in Africa). According to Ancient maps, Libya encompassed vast parts of Africa. One of the earliest world maps by Hecataeus of Miletus (c. 550–476 BCE), actually divided the world into Europe, Asia, and Libya. Africa was Libya and Libya was Africa.

The name Africa wasn't even a concept back then. Africa was the name placed on the continent later on by the Romans. Some even say that the name Africa is the name of a Yemenite chief named Africus who invaded North Africa in the second millennium B.C.E. and founded a town called Afrikyah. In addition, *Afri* was a Latin name used to refer to the inhabitants of Africa, which in its widest sense referred to all lands south of the Mediterranean (Ancient Libya)[20],[21]

---

[20] Georges, Karl Ernst (1913–1918). "Afri". In Georges, Heinrich. *Ausführliches lateinisch-deutsches Handwörterbuch* (in German) (8th ed.). Hannover. Retrieved 20 September 2015.

[21] Lewis, Charlton T.; Short, Charles (1879). "Afer". *A Latin Dictionary*. Oxford: Clarendon Press. Retrieved 20 September 2015.

A cave drawing of an Amazon woman with a pointed Cap with Bow found in Southwest Libya in the mountain area of Fezzan.

Africa as a name seems to have originally referred to a native Libyan tribe. The name is usually connected with Hebrew or Phoenician *afar* 'dust', but a 1981 hypothesis[22] has asserted that it stems from the Berber *ifri* (plural *ifran*) "cave", a reference to cave dwellers of Africa[23]. The same word may be found in the name of the Banu Ifran from Algeria and Tripolitania,

---

[22] Names of countries, Decret and Fantar, 1981
[23] Geo. Babington Michell, "The Berbers", *Journal of Royal African Society*, Vol. 2, No. 6 (January 1903), pp. 161-94.

a Berber tribe originally from Yafran (also known as *Ifrane*) in northwestern Libya[24].

Speaking of cave dwellers, in Southwest Libya, in the mountain area of Fezzan there was an interesting discovery, there were ancient rock engravings found there. In 1954 an Italian expedition (which included Paolo Grraziose, Vergara-Caffarelli and Dr Paradisi) discovered a large collection of animal engravings and female figures in rock shelters in Wadi el Kel, about 300 miles south of Tripoli[25]. Apparently, the same engravings were reported in 1874 by the explorer Rohlfs. One of these engravings shows a female person. She was wearing a pointed cap. Greek representations of Amazonian women wear very similar caps. Furthermore this figure (depicted above) is armed with a bow - a popular weapon of the Greek Amazons. Today this area is a stone desert where human life is impossible. These pictures must have been made when living

---

[24] Edward Lipinski, *Itineraria Phoenicia*, Peeters Publishers, 2004, p. 200. ISBN 90-429-1344-4
[25] Culture and Customs of Libya. By Toyin Falola, Jason Morgan, Bukola Adeyemi Oyeniyi

there was possible, long time ago. Desertification started in this region about 4000 years ago.

- ## The Sauromatians

A representation of Sauromatian women. The Sarmatian women, now called the Xiomara meaning "famous warrior", after centuries with no men had to learn to defend themselves and became formidable warriors.

One day, according to Amanda Foreman [Smithsonian], in the early 1990s, a joint U.S.-Russian team of archaeologists made an extraordinary discovery while excavating 2,000-year-old burial mounds—known as *kurgans*—outside Pokrovka, a remote Russian outpost in the southern Ural Steppes near the Kazakhstan border. There, they found over 150 graves belonging to the

Sauromatians and their descendants, the Sarmatians. Among the burials of "ordinary women," the researchers uncovered evidence of women who were anything but ordinary. There were graves of warrior women who had been buried with their weapons.

One young female, bowlegged from constant riding, lay with an iron dagger on her left side and a quiver containing 40 bronze-tipped arrows on her right. The skeleton of another female still had a bent arrowhead embedded in the cavity. Nor was it merely the presence of wounds and daggers that amazed the archaeologists. On average, the weapon-bearing females measured 5 feet 6 inches, making them preternaturally tall for their time.

Finally, here was evidence of the women warriors that could have inspired the Amazon myths. In recent years, a combination of new archaeological finds and a reappraisal of older discoveries have confirmed that Pokrovka was no anomaly. Though clearly not a matriarchal society, the ancient nomadic peoples of the steppes lived within a social order that was far more flexible and fluid than the polis of their Athenian contemporaries. Much of these finds focus much on European Amazon warrior women. But there were also women in Africa that were called Amazons post Libya.

- **Dahomey Amazons**

One of Dahomeys' women warriors, with a musket, club, dagger—and her enemy's severed head. From Forbes, Dahomy and the Dahomans (1851).

Missionary Francesco Borghero, in the fall of 1861, documented that he encountered a tribe of West African Women Amazons[26]. The Dahomey Amazons or Mino was an all-female military regiment of the Fon people of

---

[26] Dahomey Women Warriors, By Mike Dash, Smithsinian.com, Sept.23, 2011

the Kingdom of Dahomey in the present-day Republic of Benin[27]. While European narratives refer to the women soldiers as "Amazons," because of their similarity to the semi-mythical Amazons of ancient Anatolia, they called themselves Ahosi (king's wives) or Mino (our mothers) in the Fon language.

In 1890, King Behanzin used his Mino fighters alongside the male soldiers to battle the French forces during the first Franco-Dahomean War. The French army lost several battles to them because of the female warriors' skill in battle. The European general that led an assault against the Dahomey people compared the valor of Dahomey's women warrior elite to that of European troops and suggested that such equally brave peoples should never be enemies.

We just can't say that the Dahomey women were an anomaly, when warrior type women are found worldwide is my point. If they existed in other cultures, they must have

---

[27] Atlantic Black Star : 10 Fearless Black Female Warriors Throughout History. By A. Moore- Oct 29, 2013,

existed in the mother culture, where mankind originated, from mother Africa. Because there existed African Women Pharaohs like Twosret, Hatshepsut, Nefertiti, Sobekneferu and MerNeith were women of antiquity to reign during Egypt's long history. There existed women like the Kushite Queen Amanirenas (40 BC) who led an army of 30,000 men against Emperor Augustus Roman army in the Egyptian city of Aswan. Famous Greek historian, Herodotus, wrote of the Libyan tribes, referring to the Zavecians, *"whose wives drive their chariots to battle,"* Then you have the testimony of another Greek Historian Diodorus Siculus that states that the original Amazons came from African-Libyan women. Amazons existed, although some of the stories grew to a mythological scale. How else would you explain being defeated by women? They had to have had superhuman abilities with super powers?

- **The Damute and Gorage Amazons**

There were other African Amazonian women besides the Dahomey women. As late as 1840, M. d'Arnaud found the king of the

Behrs surrounded by a body of speared carrying women. It was somewhere in this neighborhood that Father Alvares gathered information concerning an Amazonian nation differing widely from the classical type. The father accompanied the Portuguese Ambassador to the Court of Prester John, Emperor of Abyssinia in 1520-1527, and in his quaintly straightforward narrative of the mission, he gives an account of the tributary kingdoms of Damute and Gorage, which lay to the south-west of Prester John's territories. After this he adds:

"They say that at the extremity of these kingdoms of Damute and Gorage, towards the south, is what may be called the kingdom of the

Amazons; but not so,--as it seems to me, or as it has been told to me, or as the book of Infante Don Pedro related or relates to us,--because these Amazons (if these are so) all have husbands generally throughout the year, and always at all times with them, and pass; their life with their husbands. They have not a king, but have a queen. She is not married, nor has she any special husband, but withal does not omit having sons and daughters, and her daughter is the heir to the kingdom. They say that they are women of a very warlike disposition, and they fight riding on certain animals, light, strong, and agile, like cows, and are great archers; and when they are little they dry up the left breast, in order not to impede drawing the arrow. They also say that there is very much gold in this kingdom of the Amazons, and that it comes from this country to the kingdom of Damute, and so it goes to many parts. They say that the husbands of these women are not warriors, and that their wives dispense them from it. They say that a great river has its source in the kingdom of Damute, and opposite to the Nile, because each one goes in its own direction, the Nile to Egypt: of this other no one in the country knows where it goes to, only it is presumed that it goes to Manicuigo."

Here we have sufficient details of what appears to have been a matriarchal state, peculiar in this, that the women were trained as warriors, but not Amazonian as described at Themyscira, though the drying-up of one breast is certainly suggestive of the Asiatic practice. But it is the account of a complete community, like that of the Sauromatae Gynaecocratumeni, merely with the special social functions reversed; thus it does not fall into the same class as the Grecian myth of the unnatural state, which no doubt explains the cautious hesitation of the, reverend chronicler[28].

Father Jaos dos Santos, who had preceded Alvares, visiting Abyssinia as a missionary in 1506, says:

---

[28] The Amazons by Guy Cadogan Rothery [1910], Chapter vii, Amazons of Africa, pg 109 -138

"In the neighborhood of Damute is a province in which the women are so much addicted to war and hunting that they constantly go armed. When contention fails in their neighborhood they purposely excite quarrels among themselves, that they may exercise their skill and courage, and neither the one be injured nor the other relaxed by idleness. They are much more daring than the men of the country, and that they may have no impediment to the proper exercise of their right arm, they are accustomed, while their daughters are young, to scar the breast of that side with a hot iron, and thus wither it to prevent growth. Most of the women are more occupied with warfare than the management of their domestic affairs, whence they rarely marry, and live as formerly did the Amazons of Themyscira. Where by chance any enter the marriage state and have children, they take charge of them no longer than till they are weaned, after which they send them to their fathers to be brought up. But the chief of them imitate the example of their queen, who

lives in a state of perpetual virginity, and is regarded as a deity by her subjects--nay, even all the sovereigns whose territories are adjacent to hers pride themselves on living with her on friendly terms, and defend her against any attack. Indeed, the power of this monarch is such as to make her another Queen of Sheba, whose authority over her subjects, as is related by the Patriarch Bermudes in his book on Prester John, was without limit. The same patriarch relates that off the coast of China islands are found peopled with Amazons who suffer no man among them except at certain seasons, for the preservation of the race." [Guy Cadogan Rothery. The Amazons].

This all points to a strong possibility that a warrior type woman from Africa, described by Garci Rodríguez de Montalvo called *"Las sergas de Esplandián"* (The Adventures of Esplandián), could have existed in the Americas since the so-called Africans did travel to Western lands, (according to Ivan Van Sertima.) Montalvo's novel may have influenced Father Jaos dos Santos story of Damute Amazonian Women.

- **Amazons in America**

The Island of Tumpinambaranas is the name of a former fluvial island bordered by rivers of the Amazon system (Amazon, Madeira, Sucunduri, and Abacaxis) in eastern Amazonas, Brazil.

Guy Rothery has a full chapter in his book about the Amazons in America. Rothery noted:

> "In 1540, some forty years after Allonzo Pinzon had discovered the great Marañon, Francesco de Orellana, making his way from far-off Peru to the Atlantic through the Brazils, explored the magnificent river, he and his companions meeting with many difficulties. ....but most persistent of all

were the rumors **(that they heard of while on their travels[29])** *of warrior women who lived apart from men. The grandeur and novelty of the scenes they were passing through, the weirdness of the stories they heard, all prepared the Spanish adventurers to accept the marvelous, so that when they had accomplished rather more than half of their journey, and were approaching the Trombetus River in the neighborhood of the great, densely wooded island of Tumpinambaranas, formed by the junction of the Madera with the Marañon, they found themselves opposed by warlike natives gathered on the banks, and among them noticed women seemingly acting as leaders of the men, they readily fell into the notion that here they had stumbled upon the renowned Amazons. In this belief they were confirmed by the natives whom they cross-examined, and de Orellana, duly impressed with this wonderful discovery, and some say actuated by a*

---

[29] Insertion is purely mine for clarification.

> *desire to magnify his own exploits, renamed the Marañon River the Amazon, a name subsequently given to a whole vast province.*[30]*"*

There is another account about the Amazons by the English explorer **Sir Walter Raleigh** (*circa* 1554 – 29 October 1618). In 1594, Raleigh heard of a "City of Gold" in South America and sailed to find it, publishing an account of his experiences in a book, The *Discovery of Guiana,* which contributed to the legend of "El Dorado". Sir Raleigh says that he spoke to a Native American chief that had been to the Amazon River and beyond. This chief reported that

> *"the nations of these women are on the south side of the river, in the province of Topago, and their chiefest strength and retreats are in the lands situated on the south side of the entrance, some sixty leagues within the mouth of*

---

[30] The Amazons by Guy Cadogan Rothery [1910], Chapter VIII "Amazons of America", pgs 139- 163,

> *the same river. The memories of the like women,"*

....adds the gallant knight,

> *"very ancient as well in Africa as in Asia, in many histories they are verified to have been in diverse ages and provinces, but they which are not far from Guiana do accompany men but once a year, and for the time of one month, which I gather by their relations to be April. At that time all the kings of the borders assemble and the queens of the Amazons; and after the queens have chosen, the rest cast lots for their valentines. This one month they feast, dance, and drink their wines in abundance; and the moon being done, they all depart to their own provinces. If they conceive and be delivered of a son, they return him to the father; if of a daughter, they nourish it and retain it. And as many as have daughters send unto the begetter presents, all being desirous to increase their own sex and kind; but that they cut off the right breast I do not find to be true. It was further told me that if in the wars they*

took any prisoners that they would accompany with those also at what time soever, but in the end for certain they put them to death; for they are said to be very cruel and bloodthirsty, especially to such as offer to invade their country. These Amazons have likewise great store of these plates of gold, which they recover in exchange chiefly for a kind of green stones, which the Spaniards call piedras hijadas, and we use for spleen stones: and for the disease of the stone we also esteem them. Of these I saw divers in Guiana, and commonly every cacique has one, which their wives for the most part wear, and they esteem them as great jewels." [Rothery – Amazons in America, 1910].

A Women Caliph in America?

In Garci Rodríguez de Montalvo book *"Las sergas de Esplandián"* (The Adventures of Esplandián), he calls the Amazonian African Queen Calafia. Scholars have noted that Queen Calafia's name has the etymology that comes from the Arabic word khalifa

(Islamic state leader) which is caliph in the English and califa in Spanish[31]. And Queen Calafia's monarchy was thus known as California, which means the "land of the caliph". Calafia may not have been her name proper, but because she was West African and therefore likely had an Mandinka female name like "Yahar Diouf, Aminata Marong, Sibo Savaneh, Oumil Ndiaye, or Satou Jallow". There are other documents that show that she had knowledge of the Islamic lands, hence she was known as the queen or the western Caliph. Probably one of the daughters' or grand daughters' of Mansa (sultan/king) Abu Bakari (1285-1312CE) or from his all-female royal guard. She may have been both.

- **Left Behind (in America)**

However, no woman has held the title of caliph in the lands of Islam (in the east). Therefore I propose an alternative meaning. It is NOT a reference to her as the religious or political leader, although she was a queen,

---

[31] Putnam, Ruth (1917). Herbert Ingram Priestley, ed. *California: the name.* Berkeley: University of California., p. 356

but it is a reference to how she became a queen. The word khalifa comes from the Arabic trilateral root KH. L. F[32]. And that the name Calafia is actually the Spanish version of the Arabic verb form 2 "Khallafa" which means to leave behind (passive participle) or one who is left behind. How else would you attribute an Arabic proper noun be attributed to a supposedly "pagan" leader [33] and a woman at that? In Garci Rodríguez de Montalvo's novel, Calafia is a pagan who is convinced to raise an army of women warriors and sail away from California with a large flock of trained griffins so that she can join a Muslim battle against Christians who are defending Constantinople.

With that said, just because Middle Eatern Islam was patriarchal, doesn't mean Islam in Africa followed that same path. Which means there is a possibility of a female Caliphate. Islam has been in Africa for so long, since its emergence on the Arabian

---

[32] A Concordance of the Quran, By Hanna E. Kassis, University of California Press, 1983. pg 687

[33] Pagan – a derogatory termed used by Christians to describe all people, including Muslims, who were not Christian)

peninsula, that some scholars have argued that it is a traditional African religion.[34]

Although the majority of Muslims in Africa are non-denominational Muslims, Sunni[35] or Sufi, the complexity of Islam in Africa is revealed in the various schools of thought, traditions, and voices that constantly contend for dominance in many African countries. Islam in Africa is not static and is constantly being reshaped by prevalent social, economic and political conditions.[36]

---

[34] African traditional religion in the modern world - Douglas E. Thomas page 125
[35] "Chapter 1: Religious Affiliation". *The World's Muslims: Unity and Diversity*. Pew Research Center's Religion & Public Life Project. August 9, 2012. Retrieved 4 September 2013.
[36] Hussein D. Hassan."Islam in Africa" (RS22873). Congressional Research Service (May 9, 2008). *This article incorporates text from this source, which is in the public domain.*

- **Queens of the Islamic lands**

With that said, many Muslim women have held political power, some jointly with their husbands, others independently. The best-known women rulers in the pre-modern era include **Khayzuran**, who governed the Muslim Empire under three Abbasid caliphs in the eighth century; **Malika Asma bint Shihab al-Sulayhiyya** and **Malika Arwa bint Ahmad al-Sulayhiyya**, who both held power in Yemen in the eleventh century; **Sitt al-Mulk, a Fatimid** queen of Egypt in the eleventh century; the Berber queen **Zaynab al-Nafzawiyah** (r. 1061 – 1107); two thirteenth-century Mamluk queens, **Shajar al-Durr** in Cairo and **Radiyyah** in Delhi; six Mongol queens, including **Kutlugh Khatun** (thirteenth century) and her **daughter Padishah Khatun** of the Kutlugh-Khanid dynasty; the fifteenth-century Andalusian queen **Aishah al-Hurra**, known by the Spaniards as Sultana **Madre de Boabdil** ; **Sayyida al-Hurra**, governor of Tetouán in Morocco (r. 1510 – 1542); and four seventeenth-century Indonesian queens[37].

---

[37] The Oxford Dictionary of Islam, Women and Islam, pg 339

- ## War in Constantinople

Mehmet II enters Constantinople after conquering it in 1453; being just 21 years old. – Painting by Jean Joseph Benjamin Constant

In Garci Rodríguez de Montalvo's novel, Queen Calaifa joins the Muslim armies to fight the Christians in Constantinople. Contrary to Montalvo's story, the Eastern Roman Empire, with Constantinople as its capital, was conquered by the Muslim

Ottoman Army, under the command Ottoman Sultan Mehmed II on 29th May 1453. With this conquest Ottomans became one of the most powerful empires in history, and the Eastern Roman Empire fell[38]. And when Montalvo wrote his book, the Turks were still in power so he knew better. Thus the story of Muslims defeat at Constantinople is but the fanciful wish of Montalvo.

- **The Sultanate of Women**

The women of the Ottoman's imperial harem rose into much power during and even before the sixteenth century. The harem was defined to be the women's quarter in a Muslim household. The Imperial harem (also known as the Seraglio harem) contained the combined households of the *Valide Sultan* (Queen Mother), the Sultan's favorites (*hasekis*), and the rest of his concubines (women whose main function was to entertain the Sultan in the bedchamber). It also contained all the Sultanas (daughters of the Sultan) households. Many of the

---

[38] Momigliano & Schiavone (1997), Introduction ("La Storia di Roma"), p. XXI

harem women would never see the Sultan and became the servants necessary for the daily functioning of the harem[39].

---

[39] All About Turkey © Burak Sansal 1996–2017

A Black family from Adzyubzha. Photo from the book Kovalevsky P.I. "Kavkaz (Caucasus). Volume I. The peoples of the Caucasus ", St. Petersburg. 1914

From roughly 1520, when Süleyman the Magnificent ascended to the throne, and reaching into the mid-seventeenth century is the period known as the **"sultanate of women."** [40] During this time, high-ranking women attained a large amount of political power and public importance. Aiding in domestic politics, foreign negotiations, and even serving as regents, the queen mothers and lead concubines in particular took on a great deal of political power and aided in

---

[40] Leslie P. Peirce, The Imperial Harem: Women and Sovereignty in the Ottoman Empire. Oxford: Oxford University Press, 1993, vii.

imperial legitimation in that time *[Leslie P. Peirce, The Imperial Harem: Women]*.

Numerous harem women were Caucasians, Georgians, and Abkhazians. Many of the Abkhazian women lived in the settlement Adzyubzha [*at the mouth of the Kodori River and the surrounding villages (Chlou, Pokvesh, Agdarra, and Merkulov) on the eastern coast of the Black Sea in Eastern Europe*] were of African descent. One origin story of these people is that the Afro-Adzyubzha is related to the dealings of <u>Narts</u> with certain "black-faced people" from the Horn of Africa[41]. The legendary Narts are said to have come back to the Caucasus from a long African campaign with hundreds of African escorts, who remained in Abkhazia.

If the Ottoman Empire's influence reached the Americas, there is a possibility that the **"sultanate of women"** would have extended their presence to the Americas also. They may have been LEFT BEHIND

---

[41] Archeology and Ethnography of Abkhazia, Colchis [Нарты у чернолицых людей (in Russian]

(Khallafa) to extend the Ottoman's influence there is one possibility. But this idea may be far reaching, but plausible. As stated before there were Amazonian Women in Northern Turkey called the Sauromatians.

- **The Island Paradise Filled With Gold**

Garci Rodríguez de Montalvo does not hold back when he describes Calafia's kingdom in his book "The Adventures of Esplandián" – far beyond the Indies (Montalvo does not specify East or West Indies), full of gold (but no other metals), and well-protected from invaders by tall cliffs and other geographic features. Oh, and griffins. Lots and lots of griffins, ridden by Queen Calafia's Amazon warriors and trained to tear apart any man they came across.

And the name of this wondrous place was the island of California, the "land of the Caliph." The story of an island paradise filled with gold and pearls was a recurring theme that Rodríguez de Montalvo was familiar with. In seeking new land, Spanish explorers were often led onward after hearing about a land of gold, or a land ruled by women.

Among the readers of Montalvo's tales was explorer and conquistador, Hernando Cortez (most famous for hastening the fall of the Aztec Empire and bringing Spanish influence to Mexico and the American West). He does NOT seem to have understood that *The Adventures of Esplandián* was fiction. Judging from his behavior, he seemed to think that Montalvo had written about a real place – and he was determined to find this fabled island of black Amazons decked out in gold and pearls.

After breaking apart the Aztecs and declaring himself Governor of Mexico, he funded several Spanish expeditions west, with the intention of finding California. When the leader of this expedition found Baja California, he at first believed he'd found an island. And more out of a sense of hope and optimism than anything else, he named the region 'California'.

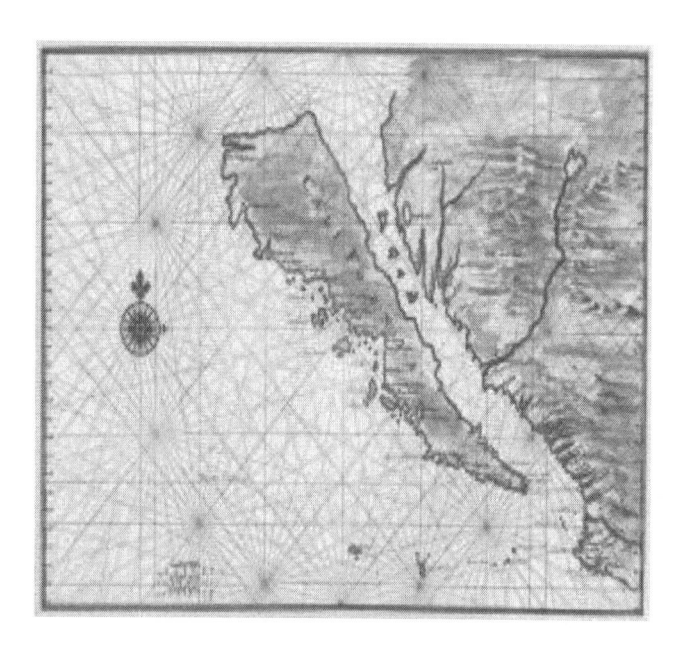

The 'island' of California.

    The name spread, with Spanish cartographers and explorers believing that the entire West Coast *must* be an island... because after all, that's how Montalvo described it! As a result, many old maps often show Baja California and California as a large island. The captain of the expedition, Fortun Ximenez, was convinced he'd found the island of the Amazons, and really, really wanted to find the gold, and the griffins. He found neither

– the griffins didn't exist, and gold wouldn't be discovered in California until 1848.

It does seem, however, that Ximenez kept wandering through California, asking the local tribes where all the women were, and was frequently told that a tribe comprised solely of women existed 'somewhere over there.' It's possible the tribes were trying to get him to go away and leave them alone (or at least go mess with their enemies), and Ximenez kept up his ultimately fruitless search for quite a while.

However, despite utterly failing to find the kingdom (queen-dom?) of Calafia, the name stuck – Spanish explorers kept labeling the area 'California' on their maps, even when cartographers finally realized the land was firmly attached to the rest of the North American continent and had nary a griffin in sight. Spanish settlers kept the name, referring to themselves as 'Californios.' And by the time the United States picked a fight with Mexico, the name had become permanently attached to the region, and California became the 31st state in 1850.

Because of this, the American state of California, Baja California in Mexico and the surrounding regions have become linked to the mythical California – despite the fact that Montalvo never really described where Calafia's island was, other than 'really far away' (using language meant to imply that you *couldn't* get to California, it was a semi-mythical place).

Mural of Queen Calafia and her Amazon warriors at the Mark Hopkins Hotel in San Francisco by Maynard Dixon and Frank Von Sloun

Since then, Calafia has evolved into a symbol for women of color, especially Hispanic, Latina and black women, living in California and the Southwest. She's become a favorite subject of folk art, often depicted as a black queen, sometimes surrounded by symbols of Californian identity.

Many Afro-centric historians wholeheartedly embrace the legend of Calafia, holding her up as a symbol of strong black womanhood and an indication that black people have lived in California for a very long time. As her legend has evolved in this context, Calafia has been described as a Moorish woman, of direct African ancestry who ruled an empire stretching from Colorado to Mexico to Oregon. The Arabic writings found by Dr. Barry Fell in those regions lend support to this notion.

- **Origins of the American Amazons**

Where did the American Amazons come from? Rothery documents:

> "Of the origin of the "women who live without husbands" a very significant legend appears to have been current along the middle and lower reaches of the Amazon. We are told that in some far-off indeterminate age the women rebelled against their husbands and retired to the hills accompanied by only one old man. They lived by their own industry, quite isolated. All daughters born to this lopsided community were carefully reared, while all boys were killed."

As I proposed before, the name Calafia is actually the Spanish version of the Arabic verb form 2 "Khallafa" which means to leave behind (passive participle) or one who is left behind. I propose that the American Amazons were the remaining troop and royal guards of Mansa Musa's brother and former Sultan of Mali, Abu Bakari (1285-1312CE) who had undertaken two expeditions into the Atlantic Ocean. Sultan Abu Bakari did not return to Timbuktu from the second voyage of 1311 CE. The Arab-Egyptian scholar Al-Umari[42] quotes Mansa Musa as follows:

> "The ruler who preceded me did not believe that it was impossible to reach the extremity of the ocean that encircles the earth (meaning Atlantic), and wanted to reach that (end) and obstinately persisted in the design. So he equipped two hundred boats full of men, like many others full of gold, water and victuals sufficient enough for several years. He ordered the chief (admiral) not to return until they had reached the extremity of the ocean, or if they had exhausted the provisions and the water. They set out. Their absence extended over a long period, and, at last, only one boat returned. On our questioning, the captain said: 'Prince, we have navigated for a long time, until we saw in the midst of the ocean as if a big river was flowing violently. My boat was the last one; others were ahead of me. As soon as any of them reached this place, it drowned in the whirlpool and never

---

[42] Al-Umari 1929, *Masalik al Absar fi Mamalik el-Amsar*, French translation by Gaudefroy-Demombynes, Paris, Paul Geuthner, 1927, pp. 59, 74-75. See also Qalqashandi, *Subh al-A'sha, V*, 294.

came out. I sailed backwards to escape this current.' But the Sultan would not believe him. He ordered two thousand boats to be equipped for him and for his men, and one thousand more for water and victuals. Then he conferred on me the regency during his absence, and departed with his men on the ocean trip, never to return nor to give a sign of life.[43]

They seem to have settled eventually in Western America. There is solid scientific evidence supporting the arrival of Muslims from North and West Africa centuries before Columbus. And as I mentioned before, Dr. Barry Fell did discover the existence of the Muslim schools at Valley of Fire (Nevada), Allan Springs (Oregon), Logomarsino (Nevada), Keyhole (California), Canyon (Nevada), Washoe and Hickison Summit Pass (Nevada), Mesa Verde (Colorado), Mimbres Valley (New Mexico) and Tipper Canoe (Indiana).

---

[43] *Mohammed Hamidullah. "Echos of What Lies Behind the 'Ocean of Fogs' in Muslim Historical Narratives". Muslim Heritage. Retrieved 27 June 2015.* (Quoting from Al-Umari 1927, *q.v.*)

And it was known that Mansa Musa used females for his royal guard, and the likelihood that his brother Abu Bakari did the same was very high. And according to Dr. Barry Fell's research, there were Arabic writings engraved on rocks in the arid western U.S, where he found texts, diagrams and charts representing the last surviving fragments of what were once a system of schools - at both an elementary and higher level. The language of instruction was North African Arabic written with old Kufic Arabic scripts. The subjects of instruction included writing, reading, arithmetic, religion, history, geography, mathematics, astronomy, and sea navigation.

This might explain how the name Calafia came to be attributed to the Queen. And California thus being "the land of the Caliph", the caliphate of Abu Bakari, and Queen Calafia may have been his successor. Perhaps there was a rebellion by Abu Bakari's people, and protected only by his female royal guard. Therefore *"women rebelled against their husbands and retired to the hills accompanied by only one old man."* That old man being Abu Bakari himself, Calafia may be a descendant of Abu Bakari, quite possibly his great, great granddaughter, thus considered the legitimate successor of the throne. So what the Spanish explorers encountered were actually the descendants of Abu Bakari Royal Guards, a few generations removed. They may have only retained remnants of their religious past thus called pagans. Just keep in mind, the kingdom of Mali had over 400 cities, towns and villages of various religions and elasticities[44]. The Female Royal Guard from Mali may have brought with them aspects of African Traditional Religions (like using Vultures in medicine), or Islam, or more than likely a hybrid of both faiths (which was a common practice in Africa[45]). Even the Muslims were regarded as pagans by the Christian explorers. Whatever the case maybe, they still retained allegiance to the

---

[44] Ki-Zerbo, Joseph: UNESCO General History of Africa, Vol. IV, Abridged Edition: Africa from the Twelfth to the Sixteenth Century, University of California Press, 1997. Pg 64

[45] A Case Study of the Effects of Superstitions and Beliefs on Mali Socioeconomic Development, by Yaya Dissa, Togo Adjouro, Aminata Traore,Aly Yorote, PhD. Scholar, School of Economics, Shanghai University, China . International Journal of African and Asian Studies www.iiste.org ISSN 2409-6938 An International Peer-reviewed Journal Vol.30, 2017

Caliphate thus joining in the war with the Muslims against Constantinople in 1453, perhaps some even becoming members of the Ottoman Turks **"sultanate of women."** The facts remain, there were Africans here in America before Columbus. And there were Amazonian type women in the western Americas.

- **<u>Mythical language of the Griffin</u>**

Griffin illustration from Lykosthenes, rare book collection, c. 1557

One of the key elements of the Calafia story is their relationship with gold and Griffins. Hernando Cortez, was intended to find both of these things, but was unable to find neither the gold nor the Griffins while in search to find this mythical California.

- **Protoceratops**

Adrienne Mayor has speculated that the discovery of Protoceratops fossils may have inspired or influenced stories of griffins.

The story about these Griffins can be found all over the world. And they may be rooted in an actual animal, a dinosaur called

Protoceratops according to the **American Museum of Natural History**[46]. The Protoceratops was a plant-eating dinosaur that walked on all four legs and had a large head, bony neck frill, and a beak like a parrot's with sharp, shearing teeth[47].

"We stopped at a low saddle between the hills. Before I could remove the keys from the ignition, Mark sang out excitedly.... Several feet away, near the very apex of the saddle, was a stunning skull and partial skeleton of a Protoceratops, *a big fellow whose beak and crooked fingers pointed west to our small outcrop, like a griffin pointing the way to a guarded treasure.... We continued to pounce on precious specimens with remarkable consistency.... Mark would sing out, 'Skull!' and, almost on cue I would find one too. The surface of the gentle slopes and shallow gullies was splattered with white patches of fossils, as if someone had*

---

[46] American Museum of Natural History, Griffin Bones. (Part of the Mythic Creatures exhibition.) - https://www.amnh.org/exhibitions/mythic-creatures/land-creatures-of-the-earth/griffin-bones/

[47] Encarta Dictionary, English (North America): Entry Pro-to-cer-a-tiops

emptied a paint can in a random fashion over the ground."

Here, American Museum of Natural History paleontologist Michael Novacek was describing the discovery of *Protoceratops* fossils on a 1993 expedition to the Gobi Desert with fellow paleontologist Mark Norell. The Gobi Desert is a vast, arid region in northern China and southern Mongolia. It's known for its dunes, mountains and rare animals such as snow leopards and Bactrian camels.

Protoceratops fossil – American Museum of Natural History Special Collections

In 2000, a historian of ancient science and a classical folklorist, Adrienne Mayor argued that the many similarities between *Protoceratops* dinosaur fossils and griffins indicate that the fossils may have influenced descriptions of the mythic creature. Mayor's first book investigated discoveries and interpretations of dinosaur and other large vertebrate fossils in classical antiquity, and presented her, now widely accepted, theory that ancient observations of the fossilized remains of dinosaurs and other extinct species influenced belief in some mythic creatures, such as the **griffin** and the **Monster of Troy**[48].

Some of the similarities between a Griffin and the Protoceratops are:

- *Protoceratops* lived from 145.5 to 65.5 million years ago.
- A beak, just like a griffin.
- Four legs, just like a griffin.
- The thin, bony frill of *Protoceratops* fossils often breaks

---

[48] e.g., Brett-Surman et al. *The Complete Dinosaur* (2012); Lieberman and Kaesler *Prehistoric Life: Evolution and the Fossil Record* (2010)

off, leaving behind small stumps, which may have been interpreted as griffin ears.
- The elongated shoulder blades of *Protoceratops* may explain why griffins are commonly said to have wings.

Although the Protoceratops has yet to be found in California, Western North America has been one of the greatest sources of dinosaur fossil finds. Scientists still routinely pull complete skeletons from digs in the Western United States, from Texas to Montana.[49]

A sedimentary rock layer called the Morrison formation is the most productive source of these fossils on the continent, and is where most of the popular dinosaurs, such as stegosaurus and brontosaurus were first found, according to the National Geographic Society.

---

[49] Where Are the Best Places To Find Dinosaur Fossils? By Molika Ashford, Life's Little Mysteries Contributor | September 24, 2010 01:59am ET. livescience.com

Dinosaur National Monument on the border of Utah and Colorado marks one piece of the Morrison stone and is a great place to start looking, but other bits of it crop up from the U.S. Southwest all the way up to Canada.

While the United States boasts the greatest number of dinosaur species found, these finds have been spread over much of the country. Canada's Dinosaur Provincial Park in Alberta wins the title of the single site with the greatest variety of species 40 distinct species among over 500 individual specimens have been uncovered there. This is one possibility why the American Amazonian were associated with Griffins. But there is another possibility.

- **Egyptian vulture**

I think that another reasonable explanation is forthcoming. A clue to this comes from the coat of Arms from the country of Mali. The coat of arms of Mali is a national emblem consisting of a circle charged with a vulture at the top, a mosque in the center flanked by two bows and arrows, and the rising sun at the bottom. Adopted thirteen years after the country gained independence from France, it has been the seal of the Republic of Mali since 1973. It is utilized on official documents as a coat of arms.

The Vulture depicted in Mali's seal comes from Mali folklore[50]. Even the heads of vultures are used in their traditional African medicine practices[51] [52].

Seal of Mali from 1961 to 1973.

Although some people want to claim that the bird symbol as a dove, to indicate the cohesiveness and harmony between the Muslims and Christians in Mali, but clearly the bird is bald and white like the Egyptian vulture. As you recall it was sultan Abu Bakari that travelled to the Americas and never returned to Mali. He and

---

[50] African Law Digest, Volume 9. African Law Center, Columbia University. 1974. p. 281.
[51] Vultures and traditional medicine. by Steve McKean 2007.
[52] USE OF SUB-SAHARAN VULTURES IN TRADITIONAL MEDICINE AND CONSERVATION AND POLICY ISSUES FOR
THE AFRICAN GREY PARROT (Psittacus erithacus), Kristina Dunn, Clemson University - 12-2010

his female Royal guard may have taken their vulture folklore with them. And the Amazonian women may have been spotted hunting the vultures for medicine and people thus associated them with the vultures. And the vultures eventually morphed into Griffin legends.

The Vulture was seen as a messenger to God by West Africans. Case in point, in the mythology of the Efik people in what is now Nigeria, Abassi was the supreme god and the father of humanity. His wife, Atai, was the mother. Abassi and Atai had two children who wanted to leave heaven and settle on Earth. Abassi was concerned that the two children would raise a warrior race that could turn against him. But Atai convinced Abassi to permit the two children to live on Earth, as long as they agreed never to work or mate. In spite of their promise, however, the children soon began to work at growing food and to mate. The Earth was soon full of their offspring. To save the world from overpopulation, Atai gave the people two gifts: argument and death. And so it is that humanity fights and dies. However, even though Abassi never visited Earth, he did not forget about humankind, which was made up of his children's children. Abassi used Ikpa Ison, a fertility goddess who took the form of a vulture to fly between heaven and Earth, to let him know what was happening below. Thus, good people could be rewarded and evil ones punished[53].

Although Efik are not the Malian people, this just demonstrates how important the vulture was and is to the West African people. Therefore the Amazonian Griffins were nothing more than the California Condor that live near the rocky shrub land, coniferous forests, and oak savannas. It was the Amazons, according to Rothery, that: "... *rebelled against their husbands and retired to the hills accompanied by only one old man."* Being that the California Amazons lived in or near mountainous areas, they would be associated with the vultures and condors that lived nearby. But the legends evolved into the Greek Griffins.

---

[53] Storytelling - An Encyclopedia of Mythology and Folklore, Edited by Josepha Sherman Volume One, page 2. ISBN 978-0-7656-8047-1

3. The Legacy of Calafia

Whoopi Goldberg as Calafia in Golden Dreams

A Cinematic California Adventure

- ## Calafia In Pop Culture

Well we have a state named after this Great Queen, California. In Bakersfield, CA they have a Califia Farms that produce organic food brands. Visitors going to Disney's California Adventure between 2001 and 2009 could have watched *Golden Dreams*, a film about the history of California, narrated by Whoopi Goldberg as Calafia. In addition, a wide variety of places in California have been named after her. The collection of California university resources on Latin American history and culture is called the Calafia Collection; you can visit Calafia State Park in San Diego County, or purchase wine from Calafia Cellars in Napa Valley; and even a Californian chapter of the Society for Creative Anachronism calls itself the Barony of Calafia. But Calafia's legacy even goes deeper than popular culture.

- **Calafia In Psychology**

I found it interesting that the story of the comic book version of Wonder woman has its origins in Psychological Science[54]. According

---

[54] Association for Psychological Science:" Wonder Woman's Secret Roots in Psychological Science :, June 6, 2017.
https://www.psychologicalscience.org/publications/observe

to the Association for Psychological Science, Wonder Woman's creator, William Moulton Marston, was a Physiologist who was a strong proponent of women's rights and he decided that comic books were a useful tool for showcasing a strong female role model to girls as well as boys.

"[N]ot even girls want to be girls so long as our feminine archetype lacks force, strength, power," he wrote in an article in The American Scholar.

After Wonder Woman's successful debut (first showcased in a 1941 issue of *All-Star Comics)* , a press release announced that she was in fact the creation of a prestigious Harvard scientist: "'Wonder Woman' was conceived by Dr. Marston to set up a standard among children and young people of strong, free, courageous womanhood; to combat the idea that women are inferior to men, and to inspire girls to self-confidence and achievement in athletics,

---

r/obsonline/wonder-womans-secret-roots-in-psychological-science.html#:~:text=Tags%3A,lab%20started%20by%20William%20James.&text=The%20lab%20focused%20on%20using,as%20way%20to%20detect%20lying.

occupations and professions monopolized by men" because "the only hope for civilization is the greater freedom, development and equality of women in all fields of human activity."

However, despite the intentions of the comic book creator, some parts of the world of Psychology, especially the Freudians (for example), the idea of the Amazonian woman is far more interesting in the abstract than in a pottery fragment or arrowheads.

The Amazonian myths appear to hold the key to the innermost neuroses of the Western male. In their minds, all those women sitting astride their horses, for example—

assuredly represent our inner animal appetite (in their minds) which was nothing but a phallus substitute[55]. And as for the Amazonian struggle with men, it speaks of their unresolved sexual conflict with them. Although biologically needing a man to procreate, but at the same time wanting to establish their own independence from them

However, the European fascination with these Black Amazons speaks to their inner desire for dominance over Black women and women in general , possibly expressing their inner most subconscious desire to return to the womb, (with the Black woman being the mother of all civilization.) *Womb envy* is real.

Ultimately we all desire to go back to the womb. And *Womb envy* is what psychoanalyst say denotes the envy men may feel towards a woman's role in nurturing and sustaining life. And the European male had this strong thirst for gold and women. To find

---

[55] The Amazon Women: Is There Any Truth Behind the Myth? Strong and brave, the Amazons were a force to be reckoned with in Greek mythology—but did the fierce female warriors really exist? -By Amanda Foreman,Smithsonian Magazine - April 2014

and conquer them both creates supreme validation to their manhood egos and further strengthens their white male hegemony, which they already had over their white women. And modern white feminism was a reaction to white male hegemony.

Neo-Freudian psychiatrist Karen Horney (1885–1952) proposed that men experience womb envy more powerfully than women experience penis envy, because *"men need to disparage women more than women need to disparage men"*[56]. "The facts of our true identity are that we, as Black people, are persons whose dominant genetic and historic roots extend to Africa, 'the land of the Blacks'. Africa was the birthplace of humankind and for many hundreds of centuries thereafter Africans, meaning Black people, were in the forefront of all human progress.

As the historian John Henry Clarke states, '*It can be said with a strong degree of certainty that Africa had three Golden Ages. The first two reached their climax and were in*

---

[56] Horney, Karen (1942). The collected works of Karen Horney (volume II). W.W. Norton Company, New York.

decline before Europe as a functioning entity in human society was born.'

Hence, BLACK WOMEN AND BLACK MEN ARE THE PARENTS OF THE ENTIRE FAMILY OF PEOPLE -black, brown, red, yellow and white varieties.[57]" Therefore it seems to be the interest of the White Spaniards when they came to America to*: disparage, control, and dominant Black women* because of their deep rooted psychological womb envy.

Psychoanalyst Karen Horney considered womb envy a cultural, psychosocial tendency, like the concept of penis envy, rather than an innate male psychological trait[58]. However, I beg the differ with K. Horney on that point, I believe due to the lack of melanin, it may be deeper than *"a cultural, psychosocial tendency"* but it may be in fact innate, based on Dr. Frances Cress Welsing's work on how melanin or the lack

---

[57] Dr. Frances Cress Welsing - pg 284, "Black Women Moving Towards the 21st Century"

[58] Horney, Karen (1967). Feminine Psychology. W.W. Norton Company, New York.

thereof affects behavior[59]. And that European conquest and thirst for power was based on ethnic genetic survival. To quote the creator of the Wonder woman comic book: "Frankly, Wonder Woman is psychological propaganda for the new type of woman who should, I believe, rule the world," Marston said. And Queen Calafia represented that in the flesh, not just in a White washed Comic book. And the constant battles with the Amazons in history, comic books, and myths represented their need for genetic survival by trying to dominate and control women..

Diana Prince represented White women's rebellion against male patriarchy, which today's feminism expresses politically. But white male hegemony needs to control them to guarantee their genetic survival. That is why up until 19 and 20th century could be lynched or killed for looking at a White woman. Even now, studies in several states that you would likely be sentenced to death row for killing a white woman than any other race.

---

[59] The Isis (Yssis) Papers. The keys to the Colors. By Dr Frances Cress Welsing. Third World Press, 1991

- **<u>Strong Black Womanhood</u>**

Queen Calafia's legacy is greater than these things. *She is a representation of strong black womanhood that comes from a race of all women warriors*, also an indication that Black people have lived in California for a very long time. That Black people lived in America for centuries, before Columbus. Therefore we were not all slaves or slave owners, not even part of that binary dichotomy that the dominant narrative says about our history. ….on the other hand some of us were warriors, and world travelers (pre-Columbus.) This is not to negate the legacy of slavery, heavens no. Nonetheless it does indicate that our story is not so monolithic. Hence Calafia symbolizes the ability of women in general, and Black women specifically, to determine their own destiny, using their own innate abilities and powers, not predicated on male hegemony. You can do-for-self. You do not have to take that abuse. You can compete with men in education, science, and business. You are women, you are powerful..

Hence, Queen Calafia represents our first female American Superhero, before there was such a thing as a Wonder Woman. Although Garci Rodríguez de Montalvo tried to subject her in his story describing her, but the historical facts about American Amazon women speaks to the contrary. Calafia was a womanist[60] in the fullest sense of the word. Not an imaginary princess like Diana Prince of Themyscira, but epitomize genuine queen of the Amazon, the real Wonder Women.

Because in Summary.
1.) Africans were here in Pre-Columbus America
2.) Amazonian Women originated in Africa-Libya
3.) There were Black Amazonian women here in the Americas.
4.) These Black Amazonian women were a break off of sultan Abu Bakari all female royal guard.
5.) The Griffins of the Amazons were nothing more than Vultures.

---

[60] "Womanism is a social theory based on the discovery of the limitations of the second-wave feminism movement in regards to the history and experiences of black women, and other women of marginalized groups" - wikipedia.

6.) The Island in Garci Rodríguez de Montalvo tale was not an Island at all but part of America which we call California today.
7.) Queen Calafia is a representation of strong black womanhood specifically, and the courage of all women in general to live free without the control of men.

Thank You

Thank you for going on this historical journey, to deciphering fact from fiction and getting to a more accurate picture of her. If you have young daughters, aunts, female cousins, nieces, and mothers, share this information with them. Let them them know they can accomplish anything they put their minds to. You can be successful business women, lawyers, scientists, engineers, congress persons, be the president, or even be a queen.

Hope you enjoyed the information contained in this book. Thank you again for taking the time to read it. God Bless you.

Haiku Poem

Queen

Calafia

By Marcus Allgood © 1/26/2021

O Hail to the Queen

American Royalty

She was a Black queen.

4. Other Books by the Author:

1. What Da Vinci Really Didn't Want You To Know: The Jesus Conspiracy by Marcus Allgood Oct 5, 2009
2. Everyday Islam: 365 days of living your life for Allah. (Part 1) by Ishma'il Abdul Haq Allgood | Feb 19, 2019
3. Everyday Islam: 365 days of living your life for Allah. (Book2) by Ishma'il Abdul Haq Allgood and Marcus Allgood | Aug 29, 2019
4. Black Thoughts: A collection of Floetic expressions of a Black Man in America. (Black Poetry Book 1) by Baba Ishma'Il Allgood, Marcus Allgood, et al. Feb 22, 2020
5. Revolution will not be Televised: Selected Sermons by a Black American Muslim Cleric (Black Islam Book 2) by Ishma'il Yaya, Marcus Allgood, et al. Mar 29, 2020

5 Bibliography

1. Los Angeles Times: " Prosecutors: No 'criminal liability' in controversial case of woman who died in LAPD jail cell" by Kate Mather Contact Reporter. July 10, 2017
2. Los Angeles Times: "Family questions circumstances surrounding death of woman in LAPD jail cell" by Kate Mather Contact Reporter. April 5, 2016
3. "They Came Before Columbus: The African Presence of Early America" By Ivan Van Sertima, (1976) from Random House.
4. Christopher Columbus, His Life, His Works, His Remains, together with an Essay on Peter Martyr of Anghera and Bartolomé de las Casas, the first Historians of America (two volumes, 1903)
5. Christopher Columbus The Journal - Nuova Raccolta Colombiana English Edition; Volume 1 Part 1 and Part 2, Published by Instituto Poligrafico F. Zecca Dello Stato Libreria Dello Stato, Rome, 1992

6. Ivan Van Sertima, "Evidence For An African Presence in Pre-Columbian America," in Ivan Van Sertima (ed.) <u>African Presence in Early America</u>, New Brunswick, Transaction Publishers, 1992, p.30.
7. Contact And Exchange in the Ancient World. University of Hawaii Press. Edited by Victor H. Mair, pg 250
8. The Journal of The Royal Society Interface: Tracking the long-distance dispersal of marine organisms: sensitivity to ocean model resolution. By - Nathan F. Putman, Ruoying He . Article Published 24 January 2013.DOI: 10.1098/rsif.2012.0979
9. Washington Post, World View, Muslims discovered America before Columbus, claims Turkey's Erdogan. By Ishaan Tharoor November 15, 2014
10. PRECOLUMBIAN MUSLIMS IN THE AMERICAS, By: Dr. Youssef Mroueh
11. THACHER,JOHN BOYD *Christopher Columbus*,New York 1950,P.380

12. Sabir, Wanda. "Wanda's Picks". San Francisco Bayview Nov 1, 2003.. * Interview with the curator of the African American Historical and Cultural Society Museum, John William Templeton. https://web.archive.org/web/20031101082701/http://www.sigidiart.com/Docs/WandasPicksCalifia.htm
13. CAUVET, GILES *Les Berbers de L'Amerique,*Paris 1912,P.100-101
14. COLUMBUS, FERDINAND *The Life of Admiral Christopher Columbus*,Rutgers Univ.Press, 1959, P.232
15. Putnam, Ruth (1917). Herbert Ingram Priestley, ed. California: the name. Berkeley: University of California. pg. 313

16. Lands of Promise and Despair: Chronicles of Early California, 1535–1846 edited by Rose, Marie Beebe, Robert M Senkewicz

17. The Amazon Women: Is there any truth behind the myth? Smithsonian Magazine, by Amanda Foreman April 2014

18. The Library of History of Diodorus Siculus, Book III, 52

19. Your Ultimate Palm Tree Handbook by Darla Wotherspoon

20. Georges, Karl Ernst (1913–1918). "Afri". In Georges, Heinrich. Ausführliches lateinisch-deutsches Handwörterbuch (in German) (8th ed.). Hannover. Retrieved 20 September 2015.

21. Lewis, Charlton T.; Short, Charles (1879). "Afer". A Latin Dictionary. Oxford: Clarendon Press. Retrieved 20 September 2015.

22. Names of countries, Decret and Fantar, 1981

23. Geo. Babington Michell, "The Berbers", Journal of Royal African Society, Vol. 2, No. 6 (January 1903), pp. 161–94.

24. Edward Lipinski, Itineraria Phoenicia, Peeters Publishers, 2004, p. 200. ISBN 90-429-1344-4

25. Culture and Customs of Libya. By Toyin Falola, Jason Morgan, Bukola Adeyemi Oyeniyi

26. Dahomey Women Warriors, By Mike Dash, Smithsinian.com, Sept.23, 2011

27. Atlantic Black Star : 10 Fearless Black Female Warriors Throughout History. By A. Moore- Oct 29, 2013,

28. The Amazons by Guy Cadogan Rothery [1910], Chapter vii, Amazons of Africa, pg 109 -138

29. The Amazons by Guy Cadogan Rothery [1910], Chapter VIII "Amazons of America", pgs 139-163,

30. Putnam, Ruth (1917). Herbert Ingram Priestley, ed. California: the

name. Berkeley: University of California., p. 356

31. A Concordance of the Quran, By Hanna E. Kassis, University of California Press, 1983. pg 687

32. The Oxford Dictionary of Islam, Women and Islam, pg 339

33. Momigliano & Schiavone (1997), Introduction ("La Storia di Roma"), p. XXI

34. All About Turkey © Burak Sansal 1996–2017

35. Leslie P. Peirce, The Imperial Harem: Women and Sovereignty in the Ottoman Empire. Oxford: Oxford University Press, 1993, vii.

36. Archeology and Ethnography of Abkhazia, Colchis [Нарты у чернолицых людей (in Russian]

37. Ki-Zerbo, Joseph: UNESCO General History of Africa, Vol. IV,

Abridged Edition: Africa from the Twelfth to the Sixteenth Century, University of California Press, 1997. Pg 64

38. A Case Study of the Effects of Superstitions and Beliefs on Mali Socioeconomic Development, by Yaya Dissa, Togo Adjouro, Aminata Traore,Aly Yorote, PhD. Scholar, School of Economics, Shanghai University, China . International Journal of African and Asian Studies www.iiste.org ISSN 2409-6938 An International Peer-reviewed Journal
Vol.30, 2017

39. American Museum of Natural History, Griffin Bones. (Part of the Mythic Creatures exhibition.) - https://www.amnh.org/exhibitions/mythic-creatures/land-creatures-of-the-earth/griffin-bones/

40. Encarta Dictionary, English (North America): Entry Pro-to-cer-a-tiops

41. e.g., Brett-Surman et al. The Complete Dinosaur(2012); Lieberman and Kaesler Prehistoric Life: Evolution and the Fossil Record (2010)
42. Where Are the Best Places To Find Dinosaur Fossils? By Molika Ashford, Life's Little Mysteries Contributor | September 24, 2010 01:59am ET. livescience.com

43. African Law Digest, Volume 9. African Law Center, Columbia University. 1974. p. 281.

44. Vultures and traditional medicine. by Steve McKean 2007.

45. USE OF SUB-SAHARAN VULTURES IN TRADITIONAL MEDICINE AND CONSERVATION AND POLICY ISSUES FOR
46. THE AFRICAN GREY PARROT (Psittacus erithacus), Kristina Dunn, Clemson University - 12-2010

47. Storytelling - An Encyclopedia of Mythology and Folklore,Edited by

Josepha Sherman Volume One, page 2. ISBN 978-0-7656-8047

48. Association for Psychological Science:" Wonder Woman's Secret Roots in Psychological Science :, June 6, 2017. https://www.psychologicalscience.org/publications/observer/obsonline/wonder-womans-secret-roots-in-psychological-science.html#:~:text=Tags%3A,lab%20started%20by%20William%20James.&text=The%20lab%20focused%20on%20using,as%20way%20to%20detect%20lying.

49. The Amazon Women: Is There Any Truth Behind the Myth? Strong and brave, the Amazons were a force to be reckoned with in Greek mythology—but did the fierce female warriors really exist? -By Amanda Foreman,Smithsonian Magazine - April 2014

50. Horney, Karen (1942). The collected works of Karen Horney

(volume II). W.W. Norton Company, New York.

51. Dr. Frances Cress Welsing - pg 284, "Black Women Moving Towards the 21st Century"

52. Horney, Karen (1967). Feminine Psychology. W.W. Norton Company, New York.

53. The Isis (Yssis) Papers. The keys to the Colors. By Dr Frances Cress Welsing. Third World Press, 1991

54. "Womanism is a social theory based on the discovery of the limitations of the second-wave feminism movement in regards to the history and experiences of black women, and other women of marginalized groups" - wikipedia.

Printed in Great Britain
by Amazon